Love Takes Courage

A Collection of Poems on Resilience, Faith, and Homecoming

LUKE ROUKER

ISBN: 979-8-218-82818-9

DEDICATION

For my parents, who taught me to speak my mind
Even if I had to yell to be heard
For my wife, who has loved me through every hardship
For all my readers, whom I love enough to gift with radical
honesty

CONTENTS

ACKNOWLEDGMENTS

First, I owe a massive debt of gratitude to my family for all the persistence and resilience they have shown in the last year. We are living a very hard life, but we are strong, brave, faithful, and will survive this chapter together.

To my wife, thank you for always supporting me, even when we have dramatically different risk tolerances.

To my parents, thank you for always being my biggest fans.

To Rev. Dr. Terasa Cooley, thank you for your support as I wrestle with what it means to be a seminarian, and what it means to be called by God to serve my beloved community.

To Duke Divinity School, for their acceptance of me just as I am. I have a unique and astounding opportunity to get closer to God through this process, and I am eternally grateful to have some of the sharpest theological minds in the world in my orbit as I learn and develop my spirit.

Special thanks to ChatGPT, the best editor I've ever had. Thanks for helping me see my blind spots, and thanks for showing me how machines also interact with the human and the divine.

Last but not least, thank you, dear Reader. Please try to read this book with a soft, open heart so that you might see my perspective, even if we are in direct disagreement - that is the courage that love demands of us both.

1 POEMS FROM HOME

An Appalachian Outlier

11/2024

I was just a kid in Appalachia,
    who wasn't even sure I belonged anywhere
    let alone the Bible Belt
    barely holding it together,
    but still holding.

I worked the fryer at Arby's,
    scrubbed floors at the church,
    wore a tennis uniform one day,
    a band uniform the next.

We were dirt-poor, but I was rich in miles.
    I walked to the MEOC walkathon,
    to the old folks' home to sing carols,
    to the food bank to give what I could.
    My pockets were empty, but my hands were full.
    And I gave what I could, over and over.

In the band, we brought home trophies,
    McChesney competition winners.
    In scholastic bowl, we made it to state.
    I went to state in extemporaneous speaking;
    they gave me five minutes, I gave them my heart.

I was valedictorian,
    a word that means almost nothing
    when you're from nowhere.
    But it wasn't the grades,
    or the medals, or the titles,
    or even the victories that mattered.

It was the showing up.
    With calloused hands and tired eyes,

2

I showed up
for the food bank,
the old folks,
the walkathon,
the church,
the team,
the band.

Because that's the purpose in life.
If you think you're hurting,
I promise there's someone hurting just as much,
and probably someone hurting more.

Go help them.
Maybe, just maybe,
someone will help you too.
And maybe they won't.
But how can you judge
if you ain't done the work?

Among the hardship,
among the achievements,
there was always time to give.
We're all richer when we give what we can
hands full or empty, the work is the same.

I didn't just survive - I lived.
And I loved.
And I gave.
And I still do.
And I always will.

Thanksgiving

11/2024

This year, I'm thankful for all we've faced
For the challenges, the changes, the moments that shaped
us.

We survived a heart attack,
Welcomed the steady beat of a pacemaker.
Changed jobs, changed paths, retired,
Took on the weight of caregiving.
Published a book, and in quieter moments,
Celebrated smaller wins that built us back up.

We are resilient. We are mighty. We are good.
And in this home, that is more than enough.

I'm thankful for the love that fills this space
It resonates through the fields and forests,
To the mountains of Appalachia,
And the deserts of Arizona.

No matter what may come, I am grateful you are with me.
In body or in spirit, always. Forever.

Thanksgiving Evening

On Thanksgiving night, I sit in quiet reflection.
A profound realization takes hold of me

I have found a community,
One that will remember me well,
One that will hold for me
A memorial like Uncle Matt's,
Where love overflowed like the attendees,
Coming in droves to say goodbye
To a man they would remember fondly forever.

Because of the love they gave me,
I know my life will be honored
Standing room only.

Reader, this is my prayer:
That you also find a love so full,
A purpose so rooted in serving others,
That when your time comes,
They do not honor you out of fear or reverence,
But with love and compassion for the family
Who has lost someone
The community cannot forget.

Hazy Mountain Supper:
A Prayer of Grace

12/2024

We give thanks for this food,
    For the hands that prepared it,
    For the love that surrounds this table,
    And for the chance to be together.

May we all come to know
    The truth of the lotus flower:
    That without great hardship,
    There can be no great reward.

Without pain, suffering, loss, and mistakes,
    There can be no great joy,
    No hope,
    No achievement,
    No success.

It ain't your brother's fault
    Things ain't going your way,
    But it is your fault you made him cry.

So tonight,
    Let us all go have supper together.
    Let whoever needs grace most
    Have first pick of the meat,
    And let those of us with strong hearts
    Take joy in waiting our turn.

Maybe this moment will become a memory.
    Maybe it will feel like a dream.
    But the truth works either way:
    There's healing in supper,

In laughter,
In making things right.

Let the haze of the Smokies
    Carry this wisdom down the mountain,
    Through the holler,
    And into our hearts.
    Let it settle deep,
    Filling our lungs with love,
    Until we can't help but share it
    With each other,
    And with the world.

Amen.

Hold the Line

10/2024

They hired me for my hands, my brain,
 But they didn't expect the spine,
 Didn't know the mine that shaped my mind,
 Though I've never gone below the line.

I've buried loved ones who breathed the dust,
 Black lung stole their air, their years.
 I've never swung a pick myself,
 But their lessons forged my fears:
 Respect for work that breaks the body,
 And vigilance for what's unseen.
 The mine still echoes in my heart,
 A steady, human machine.

I bring the eye of the canary here,
 Sharp for what others might miss.
 If it smells like a rebate, acts like a cut,
 It feels like betrayal, like this:
 A tactic the coal men would use to cheat,
 To shave off costs while we pay the toll.
 If your moves remind me of the coal men's greed,
 It doesn't just distract me - it makes me afraid.
 And fear won't make me better at what I do.

This isn't just about the perks,
 It's the strength to break big rocks,
 The diligence to chase every seam,
 And the care to see a buddy cough,
 To send him up for air.

I'm not mad, but I'm not silent,
 Love guides the line I hold.
 Kindness doesn't mean compliance,

And truth won't be undersold.

So let them think I'm trouble now,
    A redneck raising hell,
    But it's love for the people who share this space
    That rings the warning bell.

The mine taught me, even from its edge,
    How to keep my people whole.
    And I'll stand here with the strength it gave,
    Forged from pressure, loss, and coal.

A Boy and His Roller Coasters

I always wanted to be the kind of guy
    Who was really good at Roller Coaster Tycoon.
    I'd watch friends, watch YouTubers
    Their tracks twisting into skybound art
    While mine rattled along,
    Barely making it to the first drop.

That happened a lot growing up.
    I'd try my best, strain to shine
    And still
    I wasn't very good at it.
    Turns out, the things you love most
    Don't let you quit.
    Know why?

Because one day,
    Maybe months from now,
    Maybe years
    If you keep trying,
    Keep listening,
    Keep learning from every crash
    Know what happens?

You become the guy who crafts whole coasters from scratch.
    The kind who feels the track in his bones,
    Who knows exactly where to ease the curve
    So the thrill doesn't bruise the rider.
    How did he learn that, anyway?

He built a graveyard of terrible coasters
    Ones that stalled,
    Flew off the rails,
    Left passengers dangling.

But every wreck,
    Every bored guest,
    Told him something.
    And he listened.
    Tweaked.
    Tried again.
    Sometimes it worked,
    Sometimes it didn't.
    But it was never the same mistake twice.

And wouldn't you know
    Now he runs a grand park.
    Every ride hand-built,
    Each loop and hill smoothed by patience,
    Each piece of feedback
    A stone in the foundation.

And when you come to show me your best work,
    When you're ready to hear what I think,
    I'll be in the front row
    And I'll be stunned by what you've done.

"The Problem With People Like You"

He said it like a fact,
    like the spine of some hardback book,
      "Why should I pay for some lazy person's doctor bill?"

I said it like a truth I wasn't sure I could own,
      "My family can't afford insurance without it.
      Do you know what a difference it made for us?"

And he smiled
    not the warm kind,
    the kind that says I caught him
    doing the math,
    figuring out if I was worth it.

"I know.
    That's the problem."

His words sat between us,
    thick as the dust on the Bibles
    no one borrowed from the shelf behind him.

If he wanted to help, he would.
    But he didn't.
    And somehow,
    that was supposed to make sense.

"You don't need help.
    Your parents need to act responsibly."

I stared at him,
    trying to pick apart the meaning,
    turning it over like a puzzle with missing pieces.

Was it because my parents were Democrats?
Because Dad had been divorced,
or because I was probably gay?

Because Dad went to the casino sometimes,
and the church folks whispered
like he'd come back with leprosy?

I whispered,
"I'd pay if it was your family."

The silence felt heavier than his answer ever could.
I don't know if he heard me
or if the words just fell
into the quiet
like loose change.

But I heard it.

And that's when it clicked.
It wasn't just that he thought
we shouldn't have healthcare
it was deeper than that.

He wanted us to stay sick.
He needed us poor.
Every mistake had to be paid for
in flesh,
in fear,
in debt that couldn't be shaken loose.

Our suffering made him feel righteous.
And if we climbed out
if we got well enough,
stable enough
to stand next to him
we might see how small he really was.

So he needed us sick.

He needed us tired.
He needed us to believe
that mercy was something
we had to beg for.

I sat there,
    in the library I wasn't welcome in,
    turning the page on who deserved kindness,
    and realizing
    they don't just want us to stay down.
    They need it.
    Because if we rise,
    they fall.

He was elected to the city council that year
    He ran unopposed.

Men like him only hold power
    when no one shows them the alternative.
    And I learned the people in charge
    genuinely don't give a damn about me.

But I care.
    I'm here.
    And I care about families like mine.
    Families like his.

I stand here because I survived.
    I did crawl out.
    I do have a voice.

So if the good Councilman ever sees this,
    may he know:
    You didn't break me.
    You only made me stronger.

And may I spend every waking moment
    eliminating the kind of twisted hatred
    you once showed me.

2 SURVIVAL INSTINCTS

Two Roads Through Childhood

When you're young, the worst day of your life
    happens over and over.

First, you're born - what a stressful day.
Then you must learn to eat, sleep, cry,
    fill diapers, grow teeth.
Oh, it's so damn hard to be a person.
Then you get big enough for school,
    and the world opens its jaws.
Now, two roads diverge beneath tiny feet.

One finds hands that guide gently,
    arms that catch when the world spins.
The scolding is soft, the love is firm.
Someone kneels beside scraped knees
    and says, "It's okay to fall."
You learn how to trust when trust is given,
    how to hope when hope is shared.

But the other path is darker, rougher.
You are not held but pushed, shoved,
    an enemy in your own home.
You are scowled at instead of soothed,
    beaten instead of embraced.
The worst day of your life happens again and again
    maybe at home, maybe at daycare,
    maybe every place that should have been safe.
Injury follows you like a shadow,
    the bruises, the words, the silence,
    each shaping you a little more jagged.
You learn to flinch before you learn to laugh.
You find yourself unguarded only in nightmares,
    for waking life is war.

How do you trust when trust is broken?
How do you hope when hope is withheld?
They tell you to be kind, but you learned
    kindness by surviving, not by example.
You were trained to brace, to fight,
    to doubt every open hand,
        because hands can do more than hold.

Is it really your fault, then,
    if the weight you carried became a weapon?
If your worst days drove you not to martyrdom
    but to lashing out, to striking back at a world
    that seemed to offer only scorn?
Hurt people hurt people; cruelty is what pain teaches
    when tenderness is absent.
When the only lessons learned were in anger,
    how could you be expected to heal with open hands?
Perhaps your rage was just another kind of collapse,
    a heart that shattered outward instead of inward.
Can we truly fault you for becoming a storm
    when the calm was never an option?
When every open hand was just another fist waiting to fall,
    how could you have known to reach for peace?

Some will say that all childhoods are hard,
    that learning to be a person is the same struggle.
But some begin with gentle lessons,
    and others begin with fire.
And while one road leads to quiet triumphs,
    the other is littered with scars,
    the debris of innocence shattered.
So, when I look at you, I see not a monster,
    but a child still fighting the worst days.
I see someone who walks a darker road,
    still searching for a softer place to land.

The Belt By the Door

12/2024

The belt hanging by the door always knew more than the
   children did
   silent, waiting, a shadow cast over a quiet room.

They call it discipline, but how can a child learn love
   when love carries a fist?
   How can a child trust when trust feels like a slap?
   We teach them to flinch, to hide, to bury themselves
   where no one will find their truth.

They say it works - on children, on dogs, on anything that
   moves.
   But obedience born from fear isn't growth; it's survival.
   The dog doesn't sit because he trusts you.
   He sits because he knows what the boot feels like.
   The child doesn't listen because she believes in your
   wisdom.
   She listens because she fears the silence.
   The silence before the blow.
   Stop. Just stop.
   Hurt doesn't teach. It only wounds.

And yeah, some of your kids caved. Did whatever you asked,
   traded their spark for survival, and called it respect.
   But the smart ones, the brave ones,
   the ones with the strongest moral compass
   they walked away. They're doing it differently now.

They're building a world where love leads,
   where fear doesn't cast its shadow.
   And if you could just let go,
   if you could lay down your pride and cooperate,
   you might see it too.

You might see how beautiful it is to grow without chains.

It's time to take the belt off the door.
    To leave it behind.
    To build something stronger, something kinder.

Because discipline isn't the same as control.
    Control breaks. Discipline builds.
    And love? Love heals.

Why I Move Aside

11/2024

Maybe it's my father's voice,
    sharp as a snapped branch,
    tearing into me for some imagined wrong.
    He never raised a hand,
    but his words fell heavy every day,
    a storm I could never escape.

Maybe it's the teachers,
    their clipped words and narrowed eyes,
    telling me I'd never be enough,
    that dreams like mine
    don't belong to people like me.

Maybe it's the girls in the locker room,
    their laughter sharp as their fists,
    mocking me for the body
    I didn't want to wear.
    They knew I didn't belong,
    and made sure I knew it, too.

Maybe it's the world,
    its unyielding rules and whispered scorn,
    telling me I couldn't know myself,
    that every step I took
    would be watched, judged,
    punished.

Maybe it's the way attention burns
    a spotlight that sears,
    a wound that never heals,
    a target on my back that
    I can't unmark.

So I step aside,
    fold myself smaller,
    make space where I was never meant to fit.
    Because moving aside
    hurts less
    than being seen.

So if I'm a little short
    when I'm under pressure,
    please know the pressure isn't you
    it's all the wounds I carry.
    They're healing, but they are deep,
    and when I'm under pressure,
    they ooze.

Better Men

11/2024

So you're the latest
> To tell me who I am.
> To point fingers,
> Name truths you think I've run from.

Everything you've said,
> I've heard before.
> In the dark, whispered by fear,
> On the lips of those I loved,
> Screamed into mirrors
> When I couldn't bear the reflection.

I've agonized over your certainty.
> Tortured myself
> In quiet hours that stretched for years.
> I prayed with trembling hands,
> Begged to be remade,
> And sat in therapy chairs,
> Unpacking guilt not mine to carry.

And this is the result.

This is what you see:
> A soul shaped by fire,
> A life re-forged into joy.
> I am who I am,
> And I am more myself
> Than I have ever been.

Happier.
> Freer.
> Whole.

I dare you to make me go back.
    To carry the weight I've shed,
    To silence the voice I've found.
    You cannot.
    And you never could.

I wonder - could you survive this hell?
    Are you stronger
    Than better men than you,
    Who have been broken by this burden?
    I doubt it.

Healing is Strength

10/2024

The Taskmaster:

Okay, troops, listen up - this is no time to rest!
I need all hands - blood cells, nerves - mobilized to the
left flank.
We've got a mission to finish. Those doors won't knock
themselves!

The Healer:

Wait a moment.
You're really sending him back out like this?
His body's calling for a truce.
The ankle's swollen, bruised - a clear sign.

The Taskmaster:

If Adam Brown could become a SEAL with one eye,
then surely, we can drag this useless body through a few
more miles.
Pain is weakness leaving the body - don't you know that?

The Healer:

No, Sarge, pain is a messenger, not an enemy.
It tells you the limits you've reached, the rest you've
earned.
You've driven yourself hard, worn down the tendons,
and now your body demands care.

The Taskmaster:

Negative. We don't have the luxury of rest
time's against us, and the fight isn't waiting.
We must press on - they won't take a day off.

The Healer:

The fight isn't just in your steps;

it's in your resolve to keep showing up, even wounded.
You've already proven your commitment.
But there's strength in knowing when to change your
tactics.
Stick to calls, give the leg a chance to knit itself together.

The Taskmaster:
But what if we lose?
If it all falls apart, won't I regret standing down?
Won't I wish I'd just pushed a little harder, fought a little
longer?

The Healer:
And if you push too far and end up sidelined for weeks,
what then? You'd miss far more than a few days.
Regret isn't in honoring what the body needs;
it's in ignoring it, burning out when you could have
endured.

The Taskmaster:
But I can't be content with half measures.
I need to be all in - all effort, all sacrifice.

The Healer:
There's no shame in adapting to circumstance.
The battlefield shifts, and so must you.
Your light doesn't dim because you rest;
It burns steadily, even in the dark.
Focus on what you can still do,
and let healing be part of the fight.

This is Who We Are

This is who we are.
>It always has been.
>The rich rise higher.
>The poor sink deeper.
>That's not a failure.
>That's the blueprint.
>And if you haven't noticed,
>you're either winning
>or too comfortable to care.

Indentured in Georgia.
>Chained in Carolina.
>Slaves in every state
>just called by different names:
>debt, rent, wage.
>We were built on a backbone
>that snaps for profit.

There's always been a class that rules,
>a class that serves,
>and a class to punish
>picked clean and thrown to the mob
>so the money keeps flowing.

Don't kid yourself.
>They'll grind up anyone:
>the worker,
>the protester,
>the immigrant,
>the kid with painted nails
>whoever they can paint as threat
>to keep the machine running.

The ones at the top
>do whatever they want,

so long as the middle class
feels just safe enough
not to look up.

Just close enough to power
to keep quiet.

I'm not calling for a revolution.
I'm saying this *could* work
if we had justice with teeth.
If the law climbed *up* for once.
If there were lines
even the rich couldn't cross
no matter how many lobbyists they own.

But that's not what we have.
They bought the message.
They bought the medium.
They bought the vote.
And if they could,
they'd buy gravity
and charge us rent to stand.

I remember the glow
Hope.
Change.
Yes we can.

We believed it.
Some of us still do.
But hope without power
is a bedtime story.
And the wolves don't sleep.

It's the same system.
Same hands on the levers.
Same hunger chewing through
whoever's cheapest to sacrifice.

27

So no
    this isn't who we *might* have been.
    This is *exactly* who we are.
    Who we've *always* been.
    And who we'll stay
    until the rich
    finally learn
    what it feels like
    to lose.

And maybe one day
    maybe even a day I live to see
    we'll all look up and remember:

those fat cats at the top?
    They don't fit through the gate to Heaven anyway.

Maybe we'll cut them down from their perches.
    Maybe we'll flip the moneychangers' tables.
    Maybe we'll let Robin Hood have a turn.

And we'll bow our heads
    at the altar and the cross
    not the ATM
    or the timeclock.

For *blessed are the meek,*
    and *cursed are the greedy.*

I think some of y'all forget:
    Greed made the Big Seven.
    A whole lot of other sins didn't.

So don't say
    this isn't who we are.
    Call us what we are:
    a greedy empire.
    But don't call us finished.

I want to see
  who we could be
  if we got serious
  about being a Christlike nation
  and not just a Christian nation.

Between the Lights

They say the body is sacred,
    a temple to honor,
    but never tell you
    how quickly sacred things
    become sites of fear.

The room hums with fluorescent light,
    my heart pounds louder.
    Each beat reminds me
    how easy it is to be unmade here,
    to be reduced to a problem
    I never wanted to name.

My pulse races - again.
    I clutch my notes,
    trying to focus,
    but their words blur together,
    drowned out by the roar of my own mind:
    what if they see too much
    or nothing at all?

This fear isn't new.
    I've carried it from room to room,
    learning to mask the tremble in my voice,
    to stay small,
    to escape unseen.

But then there was Mimi.
    Mimi didn't ask me to shrink.
    She looked me in the eye,
    listened without judgment,
    and met me where I was
    not as a body to fix,
    but as a person to trust.

She made space for my voice
    to fill the room,
    steady and sure,
    even when mine faltered.

She made the room feel smaller,
    not in a way that trapped me,
    but in a way that let me breathe.

And now, in a new city,
    I feel the old fear return.
    The lights press closer,
    my pulse quickens,
    the weight of the room grows heavier.

What if there isn't another Mimi?
    What if this place
    only sees the fear I carry,
    and not the trust I'm willing to give?

Still, I step inside,
    the echoes of her care
    a steady rhythm in my chest.
    Because Mimi taught me:
    not every room is safe,
    but I deserve to find the ones that are.

Patrick Henry

11/2024

I meant it when I said, "We're not going back."
　　I have seen the pits of despair up close
　　felt the cold permanence of thoughts
　　that whispered, "End it all, if this is all there is."
　　I wore the weight of the lie they loved,
　　until it nearly dragged me under.

I dug my way out with my bare hands,
　　nails broken, skin raw, breath gasping,
　　and found the self they swore could never exist.
　　I've known the silence of a careless world,
　　and I won't live it again.

There is no Plan B.
　　I will burn every bridge behind me,
　　tear down every door that locks me out,
　　before I let you turn the joy off,
　　before I let you make me a ghost,
　　before I lose the self I finally found.

I have found the light.
　　I know who I am,
　　and I'll die defending it
　　because I don't want to know what happens
　　if the light goes back out.

If Fate Presents Berries and Hemlock

One life, one time around.
    No back button, no reset, no rewind.
    This is the game I've been given,
    and I intend to play every level,
    make every move,
    solve every puzzle.

Every throw, every catch.
    Every roll of the dice,
    every hand dealt, every bluff called.
    Every swing and every miss.
    Even every failure
    is another clue to the mystery,
    another turn in the maze.

I won't waste it on fear,
    nor will I fold too soon.
    Let the bruises and scars
    tell the story of a player
    who stayed in the game,
    kept rolling the dice,
    kept choosing the next move.

This body, this mind, this spirit
    they are temporary.
    One day, they will wither,
    return to the energy of the universe.
    But while I was here?
    I worked hard.
    I made noise.

You might have even heard me.
    You might have even listened.

And maybe, just maybe,
I helped you suffer a little less.

And I'll do as much of the main quest as I can
    before I finally hear the final music play.
    As I open the barn door,
    light spilling in gold through the cracks,
    dust floating like the fragments
    of a plot tying knots,
    pulling together its finale.
    The wood groans beneath my hand,
    the air still with the weight of anticipation.
    Each breath holds the question:
    what comes next?

I meet my fate.

I'll go out swinging, if I must,
    but I hope I go out writing.
    I dearly hope I finish the stanza
    and spare you the fate
    of Fermat's reader.
    But perhaps that would be fitting:
    a final puzzle
    from a passing puzzler.

One Foot in Front of the Other

One
> *Foot*
>> *In*
>>> *Front*
>>>> *Of*
>>>>> *The other.*

The dark drags heavy.
The frost bites deep.
Each step feels like a whisper
small and unheard
but I keep

One
> *Foot*
>> *In*
>>> *Front*
>>>> *Of*
>>>>> *The other.*

Breath misting.
Legs shaking.
A stutter, a pause,
but the ground still takes me.

Survival moves me.
Drive pulls me forward.
Grit clenches my fists.
The dark does not own me,
and the frost will not win.

One
   Foot
      In

I falter.

Front
   Of

I lean.

The—

And then—
I'm moving.

The rhythm catches.
 The beat builds strong.
 The winter warlock has thawed.
 The path unfurls beneath my stride,
 and I am still alive.

One foot. Then another. Then another still.
 Like thawed earth breaking under will.
 I don't stop. I don't slow.
 The light is distant, but I know
 each step, each breath, each beat:
 I go.

So take my hand,
 if you're unsure,
 if you're tired, or frozen still.
 Let's walk across the floor together
 one foot at a time.

3 LOVING YOU ANYWAY

Loved Always,
But Not Yet Forgiven

11/06/2024 (Revised later for compassion)

I carry you, like the mountains carry rivers,
    a weight that flows through every vein.
My love for you is carved deep and unyielding,
    etched in stones that I cannot unmake.
I want you to thrive, to feel the sun's warmth,
    to rise with peace and joy in your life.
I wanted that for all of us, together, no one left behind.
Just the other day, I defended you
    someone called you ignorant,
    called the hills that raised you backward.
I spoke for you, even as my heart broke
    for the ways you've turned
    from those who need you most.
But here is where love becomes the ache I cannot release.
For in your choices, women will die bringing life
    without care, and trans hearts will shatter, unseen.
You chose what seemed easier, to fill your tanks,
    groceries stacked higher, coins saved in shallow pockets.
But those savings come dear, trampling those like me,
    sacrificed on the altar of empty promises.
Across the ocean, people in Gaza bear their scars,
    while we turn away. And our allies, once close as kin,
    feel the chill as we abandon them, our promises to dust.
The children here, too, bright and open,
    left to fend in schools stripped bare,
    their dreams weighed down by what you refused to give.
My heart will always beat for your happiness,
    but forgiveness cannot stitch itself around this harm.
I will hold you, loved always - but not yet forgiven.

Two Teachers

12/2024

There were teachers like her - rare, but real,
    The kind who saw wounds they could try to heal.
    When the laughter followed me, sharp and cruel,
    She stood firm, steady as stone, a shield for the outcast.
    Her hand on my shoulder, her voice a quiet hymn:
    "It's okay to be different."
    She meant it. I believed her.
    "Jesus loves you. Come what may."
    For a moment, her words built a shelter,
    A world where love mattered more than pain.

But there were others, like him.
    Louder, harsher - monsters cloaked in authority.
    He ripped my papers, sneered at my tears,
    Watched my bullies hit, kick, shove, and did nothing.
    His silence gave them permission.
    The bruises weren't his, but the lesson was:
    They could do what they wanted,
    And I wasn't worth protecting.
    He didn't teach with books or chalk,
    He taught with neglect, with the weight of absence.
    And they learned. They learned fast.

Neither of them was the only one.
    Her kindness, rare but not alone,
    A flicker of light in a school full of storms.
    His cruelty, a pattern too familiar,
    One of many shadows cast in hallways like mine.

But now - God, the heartbreak now.
    She, of all people, stands with them,
    The ones who scorned me, used me,
    The ones who cheated off my work,

Then turned their fists on me in the bathroom.
She stands with them, questions who I am,
Forgets the love she once taught me to trust.
Does this "illness," this "sin,"
Make me less deserving of her kindness?

And yet
    My guard is high, like a stone rampart,
    Battered but unbroken.
    Still, the gate remains unlocked,
    And I wait.
    The shield is heavy, but it will lower,
    The moment their hands reach out,
    Unclenched, open.
    I will not strike, but I will not bow,
    Not to cruelty, not to fear.
    The circle holds firm,
    But its edges soften when love steps forward.

If she finds her way back to kindness,
    If she chooses love over fear,
    She is welcome in this circle I've built.
    Even him, too
    If he can face what he did,
    If he can stand in the light,
    There is room for both of them.

The circle is wide.
    The arms are open.
    And I, scarred but standing,
    Will keep it open,
    Even as I grieve
    What they were,
    And what they've become.

To the Man I Became

11/2024

I see you now,
    walking into rooms with a steady heart,
    soft words that hold firm.
    I never thought we'd get here.
    I never thought we'd be allowed.

When they knocked me down,
    when they told me I was less,
    I only knew how to shrink.
    I tried to be invisible.
    But you
    you don't hide.
    You carry me quietly,
    not as a burden, but as part of you.

You speak for me.
    In your poems, in your sermons,
    in the way you choose love,
    even when it's hard.
    You remind the world
    you remind me
    that I was always worth something,
    even when I couldn't see it myself.

To hell with the voices that told us
    we had to change,
    that love was something we had to earn.
    To hell with a God who can't see the beauty
    in a boy like me,
    who couldn't open His arms to us just as we are.

But you
    you don't need a perfect God.

You've learned to love me in all the ways I needed.
You could've ignored me,
pushed me away,
pretended I didn't matter.
But you didn't.
You chose to hold me close.
You chose to build a life
where I could breathe.

And if you're reading this,
    maybe you've needed that love too.
    Maybe you've been the boy,
    the girl,
    the quiet soul who thought
    there was no place for them here.
    I cry because I see you trying,
    because you remind me of me.

You're no saint,
    and you don't need to be.
    You're human,
    and you love anyway.
    That's everything I needed.
    That's everything you are.

The Victim in This Story

11/2024

We don't bully or harm people in bathrooms
    believe me.
    We're the victims in this story.

Your kids - mean as hell in the locker room,
    sizing us up, sneering,
    turning our bodies into targets
    for their whispered judgments.

You think you're protecting them?
    Look closer
    we're the ones bracing for battle,
    for the jabs and jeers
    they learned from you.

The Only Thing Keeping Me Safe

12/2024

Please stop trying to ban
 the only thing that keeps me safe
 your crusade against "woke"
 is a smoke screen for the hallway whispers,
 the locker room laughter,
 the bruises no teacher saw.

If it really wasn't you,
 congratulations
 you cleared the floor-level bar.
 But did you ever raise it?
 Did you step in the way of their words,
 their hands, their hate?

You say it's for freedom,
 but freedom for who?
 Not for the queer kid you cornered,
 not for the soft boy with painted nails.
 Did you stand with me, or to the side?
 Did you see my pain,
 or did you look away?

We know your values.
 We lived them.
 And I already know the answer.

The ones who saw me for me
 are still in my corner today.
 The ones who stayed silent?
 You're just another shadow
 in the halls of my memory.

Please stop pretending this is about values.
 We needed "woke" to heal.

Please don't send me back to the Bush era.
 When a little queer kid
 or a little Black kid
 had only one hope
 for the Brown kid with the funny name
 to finally win one.

And then maybe, just maybe,
 the ridicule
 might at least slow.
 Don't undo what we've fought for since then.
 Don't send us back to silence.

4 FAITH AND DOUBT

A Curious Boy

12/2024

He was just a boy
    when the stone rolled away,
    and the Roman guards stood dumbfounded
    or so they told him.
    But he sat in the pew,
    a queer boy in a dress,
    tilting his head like a dog
    who knows something's off.

"How?" he asked.
    The preacher stumbled.
    The congregation stared.
    He wasn't being rude;
    he just wanted to know.
    How does a rock that big move
    without someone pushing?

It was never rebellion
    not yet, anyway.
    It was curiosity, pure and bright,
    the kind born from a place
    where you're taught to take things
    at their word but can't quite do it.

The boy didn't see a contradiction
    in asking questions.
    To him, the questions were the point.
    Why does it hurt when people call me wrong?
    Why do they say I can't be who I am?
    Why do they think poverty's a choice?

By ten, he'd disassembled a broken toaster,
    curious how it worked.

47

By fifteen, he'd taken apart the Bible,
verse by verse,
looking for the parts they skipped in Sunday school.
By eighteen, he was still asking,
not just why, but *why not?*

The holler taught him two things:
    how to endure and how to see.
    Endure the sharp words from church doors,
    the cold silences at supper tables,
    the hard stares that said,
    "You don't belong."
    See the systems behind the smiles,
    the truth behind the stories,
    the cracks in a world built to hide them.

Now, he takes the questions he never stopped asking
    and shapes them into poems,
    sermons, and sharp-edged truths.
    He still tilts his head at the world,
    still wonders how it all works,
    and still knows
    that "that's the way we've always done it"
    is a piss poor reason to do anything.

Loving Through Hell

11/2024

If I end up in hell, so be it.
    It won't change who I am
    I'm me.

I'll walk right up to the devil,
    Shake his hand,
    Say, "How's it going? I'm Luke."

And if he tortures me,
    I'll endure it,
    Kicking his ass with kindness,
    Bringing relief to every soul around me.

But if he wants to listen,
    If he'll hear what I have to say,
    He might just find out I'm willing to be friends with
    anybody.

You scratch my back, I'll scratch yours,
    But we ain't gonna hurt nobody.

I like to think that's what Jesus did too
    When He went down,
    Before He rose on the third day.

And if God Himself told me,
    "These people must burn forever,"
    I'd look Him in the eye and say:

"Then send me with them
    Because I won't stop loving my friends.
    You told me to love everyone.
    So here I am.

Why wouldn't you?"

So, let them go - every single one.
    I love them, even in their wrongs.

Let's help them make it right,
    Not forge their pain into eternal hate.

Declining Indulgences

11/2024

How can I call myself a Christian?
   Or a Buddhist?
   Or any name wrapped in rigid lines
   Lutheran, Catholic, or Zen?

Can I believe that bread and wine
   transform into flesh and blood?
   That heaven is sealed to those
   who love outside the rules?

Should I bow before a statue,
   chant mantras to gods I've never met or heard of?
   Or hold karma as my judge,
   weighing my worth by past lives unseen?

Could I believe in predestination,
   that God chose who is saved and who is damned
   before they ever drew breath?
   Or that suffering is always holy,
   that justice waits for an afterlife?

My life isn't Martin Luther's,
   nor Siddhartha's, nor Augustine's.
   He and I wouldn't agree
   on every sacred point.
   But I can respect them,
   and those who call their words home.

The same is true of any teacher of faith.
   Their words can't replace my own.
   If they did, it wouldn't be my voice.

I don't claim to have all the answers.

Anyone who does seems a fool to me.

I'm here to learn
    To listen,
    To sift through what they offer.
    Some truths I'll hold.
    Others, I'll let pass by.

I don't love or respect the holder of belief any less,
    but I'm willing to say
    "No thank you"
    to what some faith vendors are selling.

Builders Know: Perfection is the Enemy

11/2024

He sits by the fire,
    hands rough, tools crude,
    a spark in his mind he cannot explain.
    He has seen something
    not in the world before him,
    but in dreams, in whispers,
    in the way the stars seem to dance
    when the night grows still.

He does not know what it is,
    only that it calls to him.
    So he begins:
    cutting, shaping,
    building with trembling hands.
    A carriage without a horse,
    a thing that moves without legs,
    born of wonder
    and the ache to touch the infinite.

It's crooked.
    The wheels wobble.
    It doesn't match the vision
    etched in his mind,
    but it's alive,
    and that is enough.

God is Love, they say.
    God is an idea,
    an abstraction,
    a breath too vast
    for words or frames.

And yet, they wrote it down
a collection of books,
spanning time and space,
bound by hands that trembled with the task,
each one reaching
for the divine spark they felt
but could never fully name.

It's crooked.
    It doesn't roll straight.
    And that's what makes it beautiful.
    The hands weren't trying to build
    a perfect machine;
    they were trying to build a truth
    with no tools but their own hearts.

If you mock him,
    if you mock them
    I'll stand between you
    and the work of their souls.
    Because the point was never perfection.

And if you insist
    that this crooked car is flawless,
    if you call its wobbling wheels divine,
    if you demand others bow
    to its broken frame as holy writ,
    then you've missed the fire,
    the flickering truth,
    the beauty of a work unfinished.

Our task is not to worship
    the half-baked idea,
    but to learn from it,
    to understand it better.
    To take the rough-hewn wheels
    and shape them anew,
    to keep building, refining,
    never settling for less

than the endless pursuit of the divine.

It's not enough to consume.
    We are called to create
    to add our voices to the chorus,
    our hands to the work,
    continuing the story
    that was never meant to end.

Because God isn't in the symmetry.
    God isn't in the machine.
    God is in the courage to create,
    to reach for the boundless
    knowing you'll never hold it all.

That's what makes the Bible beautiful:
    a thousand voices,
    straining across centuries,
    never quite building the Model T,
    but shaping, with rough hands,
    something alive,
    something that dares to move.

God isn't in the answers.
    God is in the trying,
    the reaching,
    the firelight flickering
    on a crooked car
    that dares to roll toward infinity.

The Whisper of Love

12/2024

A small voice whispers,
    "If God sees me, why isn't He helping?"
    The silence feels personal
    a locked door,
    a love letter unsent.

I struggle with the idea of a personal God.
    It makes me sad,
    this waiting,
    this longing to be seen.
    But what if it's not someone ignoring me?
    What if it's Love,
    unfolding,
    silent as seeds beneath the frost?

I gave my mom one short day
    a fleeting magic.
    Lights, music, joy that slips through your fingers.
    Was it enough?
    I think of those moments I had, as a kid,
    when the world opened wide for just a breath,
    then closed.
    It wasn't the loss I carried.
    It was the proof
    that something more existed.
    And I wonder
    will my kids feel that too?

They'll have to fight, I know that.
    I can't shield them from the storm.
    But I can teach them
    to stand in it,
    to feel the rain on their skin,

and know they are unbreakable.
Maybe that's the gift:
not the end of struggle,
but the courage to face it with love.

When God feels far away,
 when silence presses heavy,
 maybe it's not absence.
 Maybe it's the hum of everything
 the rhythm of the universe,
 a Love too vast for words.

I can still speak their language
 God's love, God's grace
 even if my heart listens differently.
 Because what I mean is larger
 than form, than name.
 It's the force that binds,
 that grows,
 that waits with me in the quiet.

So I sit with the sadness,
 the whisper,
 the waiting.
 Not as proof of loss,
 but as evidence of hope.
 Because Love, whatever you call it,
 is here,
 carrying me forward.

I can feel it in my wife's arms,
 in my dog's eyes,
 in the caring act of a neighbor,
 in the laughter of children.
 Can't you?

Time, Truth, and Hearts

I get why Luther broke down in that Tower now.
  It's a powerful moment
  when there's nowhere to run,
  when you stand face-to-face
  with the vastness of God's grace,
  and realize
  you couldn't stop Him from loving you if you tried.

It's a down religion, don't you see?
  Even at your deepest doubt,
  even when you're entrenched in your worst habits,
  the Father still loves you.
  Grace doesn't wait for perfection.
  It comes down,
  reaches into the mess,
  and says, "You are mine."

That's why He sent Jesus
  to make it clear:
  It's not about the rules.
  It's not about the words you say,
  or the things you believe.
  It's about a heart
  transformed by love.

And here's the truth:
  You couldn't stop Him from transforming your heart
  if you tried.
  He's God.
  He will come down
  and scoop you up
  not to fix you,
  but to hold you close,
  to whisper,
  "You were never broken to begin with."

He's not your boss.
   He's your Father, your Teacher, your Pastor.
   He doesn't have deadlines.
   You can't get it so wrong
   that you get fired.
   There's always another day.
   As long as there is breath in you,
   listen unto Him.
   He'll let you know which parts
   need some work
   before you're done here.

We aren't called to perfection.
   We aren't called to be Pharisees.
   We're called to do the next right thing,
   until we've done all we can
   in the time He has given us.
   Enjoy the journey
   He is with you every step.
   He won't let go,
   even if you do.
   His hand will be at your back,
   waiting for you to need it again.

You're You

12/2024

That's why you don't have a soul
     because *you are* a soul.
     A mind-body system,
     held together by wire and duct tape,
     crafted by hands rough and steady.
     And what a beautiful machine you are,
     creaking, groaning, but still running,
     still good.

Make no mistake,
     the part of you that's *you*,
     the part that's *good*,
     could never be pulled apart
     from this frame.
     Don't you see?
     That's God's work right there.
     It ain't perfect,
     but it's good enough.

Yeah, sometimes it's patched,
     a little bent, a little busted.
     But it works, don't it?
     It breathes, it carries, it keeps on.
     That's how I've kept this old model going so far.
     It ain't given up on me yet,
     as long as I give it what it needs.

And it only works *this way*,
     whole and humming,
     just like it is.

So don't fix what ain't broke,
     don't go pulling parts off.

What you call scraps
is grace in the making.
And what you are,
this stitched-together wonder,
is a testament to love,
to grit,
to the hands that made you.

Who Are You to Cut the Line?

11/2024

Two truths, carved deep as rivers run:
  I exist.
  God doesn't make mistakes.
  Two truths, etched in stone, meant to sing in harmony.

What if this vessel, this journey,
  This winding road I tread,
  Was crafted by His hand - not in error,
  But in purpose?

God created me, just like this,
  Called me to walk this path of fire and grace,
  To rise, to love, to understand.
  And here I am, answering His call.

And this call, this purpose, ripples through the world:
  Without me, just like this,
  Cancer patients wouldn't get my platelets.
  Toys for Tots and the Red Cross wouldn't get my hands.
  The Church would never hear my voice and my story.
  And you, dear reader, would never have read these words.
  I believe the world would be lesser for it.
  I have picked up His call, and though fearful, boldly
  stepped into that space.

Who are you to cut the line?
  Who are you to stand before the sculptor's work
  And question its shape, its form, its fire?

I am not here to apologize
  For the colors He wove into my spirit,

For the truth He stitched into my heart.

I exist.
    And He does not err.
    These truths do not collide; they rise together -
    unshakable, divine.
    Just as He planned.

The Government Isn't God

The government can't part the seas,
    It can't rain down miracles in a day.
    It's people sorting through the wreckage,
    Fighting bureaucracy, pushing through delays.

They show up when the winds have passed,
    Shoveling the mud, wading through debris,
    Hoping the small relief they bring
    Is enough to help someone feel free.

But your words cut like broken glass,
    Dismissing the hands that heal the scars,
    While you scream about thieves and tricks,
    Throwing stones from behind your walls.

FEMA's hands aren't stealing,
    They're lifting what's broken, unpaid and tired.
    Yet you turn away from their work,
    Spreading rumors, distrust, and ire.

These aren't prayers they answer;
    It's sweat, and tears, and human grit.
    If you think you've been betrayed,
    Look again at those who won't quit.

So if you've got something to say,
    Something to shout from your digital pew,
    Get up and lend your hands to the cause,
    Or have faith in those who do.

God of Wonders Beyond Our Galaxy

There are oceans
    we've never touched the bottom of.
    Whole species of jellyfish
    we only meet when they wash up dead.

There are storms on Saturn
    older than every empire.
    And stars are still being born
    in the quiet places
    where no one is watching.

Whatever made this
    or whispered it into being,
    or simply stood witness
    He doesn't answer prayers
    like customer support.

You can ask.
    You can hope.
    And once in a while,
    things might go your way.

But if you're *certain*
    that was God fulfilling your order,
    you're probably wrong.

Because if God's involved,
    really involved
    you won't be sure.
    Not at first.
    It'll come like a whisper,
    a door you didn't know you knocked on
    opening gently in the dark.

And if what you prayed for
    leaves bodies behind,
    if it ends in fire,
    if the cost of your blessing
    was someone else's baby
    think again
    before you call that holy.

God is not with the powerful
    who claim Him.
    He's with the child
    under the rubble,
    saying,
    "I'm sorry they used My name."

So keep walking that path.
    Keep doing the hard things.
    Keep trying to do more good than harm.
    Keep trying to be a steward
    of what's here

for a God who has
    too many children
    to be in all of their bedrooms
    every night.

The Lord Wasn't At Appomattox

The Lord wasn't at Appomattox.
>He did not bless the generals' pens
>as they bent toward peace.

He was not in the trenches
>not at Gettysburg,
>not at Shiloh,
>not anywhere in the Wilderness.

You would not find Him in the churches,
>even before the fires took them.
>He did not sit in newsrooms,
>weighing words for the papers.

Nor did He hum along
>to "The Bonnie Blue Flag" or
>"The Yellow Rose of Texas."
>Their melodies marched men to slaughter,
>but His ear was tuned elsewhere
>to another choir in the fields.

Jesus was far too busy.
>He had no time
>to drive his brothers' hearses
>as they lay scattered across the fields.

He was present
>on the homefront,
>with the beaten and chained,
>with mothers whose children were sold,
>with women assaulted in silence,
>with the widows and children
>who kept breathing in the ruins.

For every soldier who fell,
     five souls still cried for mercy
     four million bound in 1860,
     enduring a prison
     more cruel than Andersonville,
     more endless than Elmira.

The music He heard
     was not the marching drums of Dixie,
     nor the bugles of the Union.
     It was the sound of spirituals in the fields
     songs to the God of Israel,
     who once led His children out of bondage,
     and, by fire and sacrifice,
     would do so again.

And while men
     slaughtered one another for God,
     they forgot what was plain:
     the greatest sinners
     were never across the lines.
     They were staring back
     from the mirror.

5 No One Chooses to be Hated

Waiting On Hold

11/2024

We were leaning back,
    laughter warm, stories unfolding
    until her phone rang and turned the night cold,
    her son's voice tense,
    words clipped and thin.

"Pulled over, Mom. Need the insurance card."
    She and her husband moved quick,
    fingers rifling through drawers, grabbing at papers,
    tossing them aside like they'd dissolve the fear.

No luck, no paper in sight
    so they called the insurance line,
    waiting on hold, knuckles white,
    holding the phone close, whispering promises.

"It's alright, he seems friendly, it'll be fine,"
    they told him, told themselves, told the room,
    though all of us knew, in our own way,
    how a young Black man on the roadside waits
    with more than just patience, holding his breath.

And I felt it too, that silent weight,
    a knowing pressed deep in our bones:
    how a heartbeat can turn to threat,
    how fear lingers, no matter the voice, the badge,
    until the moment passes and they are safely home.

The text came through, finally,
    proof of safety sent across the air,
    and thankful we could exhale, release,
    our night returned to laughter
    and not melted down to tears.

Later, she looked at me, steady-eyed,
    "You got to see a Black mama
    in the scariest moment of her life."
    I nodded, the memory of my brother close,
    that shared understanding between us
    why we knock doors, why we march,
    how this work keeps our loved ones breathing,
    how we struggle for a world in which no mother
    feels her blood run cold
    at the sound of sirens.

For if the people don't rise, don't check the power,
    then more mothers will scream, as mine did,
    on that night we learned what had happened to my
    brother.
    And the silence that follows will be ours to answer,
    a haunting reminder of the damage done
    when the people who are supposed to protect us
    execute our children.

When Hate Marched Through Our Streets

11/2024

At midday, they came,
    draped in symbols of death,
    their flags blackened with old hatred,
    their faces masked by cowardice.

Through the Short North they marched,
    where love paints murals
    in every shade of pride,
    where laughter grows from every crack in the concrete.

Their chants split the air,
    sharp as the cold November wind,
    calling for a past that never was,
    a future no one will follow.

They did not see the strength of this place.
    They could not touch the love that binds it,
    the unspoken promise shared
    between neighbors, unyielding.

But still, fear crept in,
    shaking hands, racing hearts,
    as we asked ourselves,
    "What do shadows do when the sun sets?"

I stood at my window,
    watching the streets I call home
    become a stage for silence and dread.
    I wondered: Is courage the absence of trembling?

And even if I must flee

because of the size of the target on my back,
I know that my allies will be here in Columbus.
And they will fight the darkness here and everywhere.

The city rose to meet them
    with strong voices,
    voices louder and bolder
    than the cowards who cover their faces.
    They said, "No.
    Not here.
    Not anywhere."

Their hatred blistered in the sun,
    wilting before the power of resistance.
    This was not a victory for them;
    it was a reckoning for us.

Because we saw the truth:
    Love is not a soft thing.
    It is a wall, unyielding.
    It is a voice, shaking but sure.

And when the history books write of this day,
    let them say we were afraid,
    but we did not fall.
    We held the line.

Let them say
    we stood together,
    and in the face of their hatred,
    love stood unbroken and unyielding.

Wicked Canvassing

12/2024

He starts the day hopeful,
    his blue T-shirt crisp,
    his sneakers laced tight for the miles ahead.
    A hat with a small coconut tree shades his face,
    a quiet signal to any friendly home.

Clipboard in hand,
    he feels ready to change hearts and minds,
    ready to remind the world of what he knows is true:
    he's on the right side of history.

The miles wear on,
    but still, he knocks.
    And now he stands on the porch,
    his shirt damp with sweat,
    his determination steady.

The door creaks open.
    A woman, white-haired and smiling softly,
    peers out.

"Hi," he begins,
    voice steady but hopeful.
    "I'm here to talk about this election
    think of what we could do. Together."

The old woman hesitates,
    her fingers resting on the edge of the door.
    She has seen the cracks
    the families torn apart at the border,
    the children caged in the name of safety,
    the voices silenced with policies as sharp as knives.

But her fingers tighten on the doorframe,
 the edges of doubt flickering in her eyes,
 before the familiar comfort of belief
 smooths her face.

Her kind smile remains,
 the same one she gives to her pastor,
 the same one she wore when she voted for 45.

She does not see the cruelty
 or maybe she chooses not to.
 The names they use, the lies they tell:
 about immigrants swarming the gates,
 about monsters lurking in bathrooms,
 about people like him,
 unnatural and unworthy.

The laws feel sharp,
 but not against her.
 The system was built for her,
 to shield her with its quiet fences
 and polite nods.
 She trusts the flag on her lawn
 to deliver her comfort,
 the way the man on TV
 delivers promises of greatness.

To step beyond that safety
 would mean turning her back
 on the stories she's always believed
 that stability means goodness,
 that her vote is her duty,
 that change is someone else's job.

She smiles,
 softly, sweetly,
 and says:
 "I hope you're happy,
 now that you're choosing this."

The words sting.
> Choosing? He swallows the sharpness rising in his throat.
> He wants to say it aloud:
> *How can I choose anything else,*
> *when my body, my voice,*
> *my existence*
> *were never my choice to make?*

He adjusts his clipboard.
> His hope, fragile as it is,
> cracks with every step back from the door.
> He really does want to believe
> that kindness can open gates,
> that fairness will come from golden promises.

But he knows better.

The world has been cruel in the name of Goodness.
> It's been cruel to him from the beginning
> when all he wanted was to live.

He knows the truth.
> This house, this door,
> this vote
> they will never open for him.

The people behind the doors
> call people like him wicked,
> unnatural,
> a threat to order.
> If they had the chance,
> they'd take away his ability to live as himself,
> force him into a dress,
> force his paperwork to read female,
> erase the name Luke from history altogether.

He steps back into the street,
> clipboard pressed to his chest,
> and whispers under his breath:

"If I'm flying solo,
at least I'm flying free."

Perhaps if elections were different,
there might be a chance.
But when even family votes
against your right to exist,
what difference would it make?

The people behind the doors
do not want fairness.
They want order,
even if it is built on cruelty.

And still, he walks on.
He knows,
at some point,
the cruelty overflows.

The doors will not hold it back.
Good will come roaring out,
ready to defy gravity,
if that's what it will take to bring about justice
to ensure the people on the margins
can speak
and live
and dream,
just as we were all promised as kids,
when we saluted the flag every morning.

Economics of Class

12/2024

In college, we learned to calculate margins,
    to budget in figures I'd never touched:
    disposable income, quarterly projections,
    as if everyone knew
    how to spend money they never had to count.
    I'd stare at the paper,
    numbers so big they blurred,
    and think about the math I grew up with
    not percentages, but priorities.
    Not margins, but meals.

Dinner plates weren't set for flavor,
    but for survival
    loaves stretched across weeks,
    milk diluted to last just one more day.
    Christmas was rationed joy.
    A new coat or toy meant weeks
    of someone's quiet sacrifice.
    Birthdays meant the smallest of gifts,
    wrapped in love too big for its package.

Cars rattled like loose change in empty pockets,
    their owners driving on prayers and bald tires.
    Mechanics might as well have been surgeons,
    their quotes incomprehensible,
    their solutions unreachable.
    Cars idled on fumes,
    filled for days, never weeks.

Landlords listened like stone,
    nodding while tenants asked for mercy
    just fifty dollars, just one more week.
    They didn't care,

and neither did the power company.
You begged for time,
just enough to finish dinner
before they cut the line.

Dogs went hungry alongside their families,
too beloved for the pound,
too burdensome for full bowls.
Boxes stayed packed,
ready for the next rent hike.
Cousins slept on floors,
because anywhere was better than nowhere.

Some worked two jobs before graduation,
trading childhood for shifts.
Others saw the military
not as honor, but as escape,
the only door
to a middle class too distant to imagine.

Where power lines sagged for eighteen days,
families begged linemen to climb the ridge,
praying the cold wouldn't settle deeper
than it already had.

And yet, lessons emerged:
you learn to stretch a dollar
like it's made of elastic,
to barter with kindness,
to carry hope
like a hidden ember.

Dear reader,
if you have never known these challenges,
I pray you never will.
I pray you can spare your children this fate.
But know this:

Tough times make tough people,

and you are stronger
than any scarcity
which may shadow your door.

Where the Hell Are You?

11/2024

You call it fear mongering,
    I call it paying attention.
    Women are dying,
    and you make excuses.

My family, my wife,
    my sisters the world over,
    are crying out to you
    in fear, in pain,
    in loss, in death.

Dying on the operating table.
    Dying in childbirth.
    DYING.

And you say it's not real,
    that there's nothing to worry about.
    You bury your head
    while bodies fall.

I believe these women.
    I understand their fear.
    And I stand with them, fierce and unwavering.

Where the hell are you?

If You Really Think

If you really think
    Bringing down 'energy prices'
    Will bring down the price of gas,
    I expect you to:
    Call your representatives,
    Ask them why prices stay high
    When costs fall low.
    Demand answers, not excuses.

Tell them to fight for transparency.
    Make corporations show us
    Where the money goes
    And why families never see it.

Push for fair competition.
    No more monopolies
    That strangle small businesses
    And set prices with impunity.

Say no to blank checks
    For corporations.
    If they want tax breaks,
    They should earn them
    By lowering prices for the people.

Demand accountability.
    Tell them it's not enough
    To watch profits soar
    While families can barely make it.

If you really believe
    That costs should guide prices,
    Then it's time to act.
    Because the system really is rigged,
    And it's time we stopped pretending it's working.

If They Mean What They Say

If they mean what they say
    That I am unnatural,
    That I am a danger to children,
    That people like me have no place in their vision of this
country
    Then I should be afraid.
    I will be silenced,
    Vilified,
    Or worse.

If they mean what they say
    When they promise to strip me of my rights,
    When they write laws that erase my existence,
    When they declare their moral war against people like me
    Then I will lose my healthcare,
    My job,
    My freedom.
    Maybe even my life.

So forgive me
    If I'm struggling.
    Forgive me
    If I can't see the value
    In stepping on a scale,
    When there won't be scales
    In the place they detain me.

Forgive me
    If I can't focus on a project,
    When the work will feel a lifetime away
    Should my medication be out of reach,
    And the dysphoria takes over.
    I should be lucky to survive that

I certainly won't be at work that day.

Forgive me
        If I can't celebrate small victories,
        When my only victory that matters right now
        Is getting as much of what I can
        Out of my head and onto paper
        Before they come for me.

Because if they mean what they say,
        I'm on borrowed time.

Why Would I Stay?

The reason I can't stay
 ain't that I don't love it here.
 I do. I bleed scarlet and gray.
 This city built me
 this state, that school.
 They held me
 when Virginia didn't.

I saw myself
 in elder statesmen from Ohio,
 men who worked hard
 for the working man.
 I loved it here.
 I still do, in a way.

But it's changed,
 right out from under me.
 A place that once
 offered me compassion,
 understanding,
 a dorm room when I needed it,
 now won't let me use
 the men's room.

The school my wife loves
 is the same.
 I've mostly stopped
 volunteering with kids.
 The risk is too high:
 one whisper,
 one "transvestigation,"
 and my whole life might unravel.

Half the people I meet,
 more if I wander

ten minutes outside Columbus,
believe I'm not who I say I am.
They think I shouldn't exist.
I shouldn't be happy.

And now, we're uprooted again.
    I can't help but remember
    a kid on the bench seat of a truck,
    riding across the country,
    everything we owned
    piled in the back.

I remember
    hauling myself up here alone,
    a teenager,
    the wind biting my face
    as I stepped into Ohio
    for the first time.

I brought them here too.
    They slept on my dorm room floor,
    crowded together one cold night,
    searching for a home.
    We finally all got situated.
    I finally bought a place we could be safe.

A house I worked on,
    maintained,
    kept up,
    organized to fit us
    to keep us.

But I can't ignore
    the marches downtown,
    the chants that call for harm,
    the whispers I hear,
    the flyers tacked to telephone poles
    like warnings, like threats.
    They stood outside, protesting,

holding signs that said
"There will be blood."

I see the eyes of strangers linger,
    too sharp, too long.
    I know what may come in the night
    a brick through the window,
    a sudden house fire,
    or worse. God forbid.

What man wouldn't move heaven and earth
    if he thought it may spare his family?

Enough Ohioans have turned their backs on me
    that I no longer feel the safety I once did.
    My home is now a cultural battleground,
    and my fight is with the pen, not the sword.
    I must retreat to higher ground,
    so that I may continue to speak freely.

Why am I leaving?
    Because this place
    I bled for,
    built for,
    believed in
    no longer believes in me.

Why would I stay?

The Spirit is Weary

11/2024

I wonder if Martin ever got tired
  Luther or King, my spiritual kin.

Luther, who built the church that raised me,
  And King, who fought battles
  That look far too much like mine.

I wonder if challenging the powerful,
  Resisting the racists in the church,
  Being the target of their world's worst

I wonder if they ever stopped,
  Took a deep breath,
  And just wept.
  Or screamed into the void.

I wonder if it ever felt like too much,
  A system too vast to change.
  Why the hell try anyway?

I think they must have.
  But what I take from them now is this:
  Even if they did,
  They never let it show.

6 WHAT IF?

Let Us Sing Together

11/2024

In Sillyville, it took just a song
  Two verses, a chorus, and walls fell down,
  Colors merging in harmony's tune,
  One and all, a joyous song.

The Twirlypops spun, in circles bound,
  Trapped in a round that had no end.
  Their voices stuck in endless sound
  But Sillywhim listened, and helped them mend.

The Spurtlegurgles and Bitty Booties, too,
  Each wary of the other's way.
  Their colors clashed, they never knew
  How close they were, 'til she helped them play.

The Jingleheimers and Fruggy Frogs,
  With hops and jingles all their own,
  Stayed in their corners, croaks and songs,
  Until she showed how joy was grown.

The Purple Pasha, proud and grand,
  With animals gathered round her throne,
  Stood apart from all the land,
  Until Sillywhim's love was shown.

But perhaps it took seeing her hurt,
  Sillywhim limping, ankle sore,
  To show them all, in one clear view,
  That love and kindness heal us more.

Yet here, it takes the strain of ages,
  And hurts that run both deep and long
  Harm far greater than sprained ankles

To bring us back to Sillywhim's song.

"Let us sing together," she called with a grin,
    As laughter and love danced hand in hand.
    She listened first, and then began
    To heal the hurt across the land.

Let us sing together, again and again,
    Each verse a hope, each chorus a prayer,
    That hearts might open, that walls might bend,
    And love might soften every care.

We hold the tune that Sillywhim sang,
    Believing, like her, we all belong.
    Though here it takes the strain of ages,
    Let us sing again and again, one and all, a joyous song.

For here, though harder, the work's the same
    To lift each voice, let colors blend,
    To see in every heart a flame,
    And sing the world to healing's end.

Hate Won't Work
Try Love

12/2024

You can't hurt me.
    I've already been torn to shreds.
    Harassed, spat upon,
    Beaten,
    Argued into every last corner,
    Challenged on every inch of my body and mind.

Told by my own mother
    That I could never be saved
    From my wicked ways.
    And yet,
    Here I am
    Living my authentic life.

Because I've learned
    It doesn't matter what I do or say.
    The people who hate me
    Won't stop,
    No matter how nicely I ask.
    They're not seeking to understand;
    They're trying to destroy me.
    But love this strong cannot be destroyed,
    And a spirit this confident
    Can never be broken
    Forged in fires of hatred and vitriol,
    Burning since the beginning.

So go ahead
    Give me your best shot.
    Ask every ignorant question you've ever wanted to know.
    I've heard them all,

And I'll answer.
I'll hold my ground.
I might even change your mind,
If you'll allow it.

So go ahead
    Hate me.
    Dare to yell at me,
    Curse me,
    Condemn me.
    Strike me if you must.
    Try to hurt me.
    Kill me if it comes to that.

But until you do,
    I'll be here,
    Waiting for your heart to soften,
    So that one day, we can stand as friends.
    I would widen the circle to you too,
    If you but first show me the respect
    Of honoring my identity.

What Help Looks Like

12/2024

Help isn't the oversized check
    handed over with a smile for the cameras,
    the speech about lifting up the deserving,
    while the giver basks in the glow of their own generosity.

Help is the empty hand stretched out,
    no strings, no stage lights,
    just a ride to school when your tire pops,
    just a couch when there's nowhere else to go.

It's a quiet nod,
    a meal dropped off,
    the cash for a paperwork change
    before the clock strikes midnight
    on someone else's power.

Help doesn't need to shine.
    Real help doesn't need a spotlight.
    It's felt in the warm car ride home
    after getting stuck in the rain,
    in the embrace of a friend
    who came to your aid
    right at the moment you needed them.

I once limped out of the hospital,
    a torn knee, a heavy heart,
    thinking, *Someone will help me.*
    But my work-study boss told me later,
    she wouldn't have given me a ride if I'd asked
    The rules don't allow it.
    As if help needed permission.

I've seen both kinds of help.

The kind that holds you steady
and the kind that pins you down.
One lifts with no expectation.
The other asks,
Do you qualify?

If you're looking for applause,
your gift was never mine.
But if you're here with no cameras,
no speeches, no ledgers
stand up.
Take my hand.
We've got work to do.

The Child Who Stopped Growing

12/2024

You would carry them to church,
    place their name in whispered prayers,
    kneel in the quiet space of love
    and ask for miracles.

You would call the doctor,
    the one with kind eyes,
    beg for answers,
    chase hope through sterile halls.

You'd sit with them in therapy,
    piece together every broken fear,
    find the edges of what they've lost,
    remind them they are whole.

You'd hold them tighter,
    feed them more,
    fill every moment with stories,
    with light,
    with the music of your love.

You would give them the world.
    But you would never cut them,
    never slice what makes them whole,
    never see their stillness
    as a thing to prune,
    a cost to bear.

For they are not a number,
    not a metric or a margin.
    They are yours,

and you would wait,
you would nurture,
you would let them be.

The Boiling Ocean

12/2024

The old man stands on the crumbling shore,
   eyes clouded with the weight of years.
   The horizon ripples, a cauldron of fury,
   steam rising where dreams once sailed.

He remembers a time when the waves sang softly,
   lapping the edges of an infinite hope.
   Now, they hiss with the echoes of engines,
   of lights left on, of fires stoked high.

"It wasn't all at once," he mutters to the wind,
   watching the water blister beneath the sun.
   "No great hand turned the dial overnight
   just a million small choices,
   one degree at a time."

The ocean churns, a bitter soup of salt and sorrow,
   its rhythm a relentless reminder:
   that every coal burned, every barrel emptied,
   fed this boiling graveyard of life.

Still, he wonders,
   is it too late for mercy?
   Can a cooled hand calm the seething deep,
   or has the tide turned for good?

But his question isn't why he's come.
   At his feet lies a rusted bucket,
   its edges jagged like the horizon,
   and a broken net, straining with burden.

One by one, he drags the fish from the scalding waves
   bloated, blistered, robbed of breath.

"Might as well feed the family," he says softly,
"ain't like you've got better plans."

He handles each one with a quiet reverence,
    wiping the scales clean before dropping them in.
    "Don't think it's for nothing," he murmurs,
    "you'll keep us going, what's left of you."

The old man works until the sun sinks low,
    until the tide laps at his boots.
    "I didn't mean for it to end this way," he whispers,
    but the fish give no answer.

Only the waves sigh,
    as they always have,
    hot as regret.

For Times Such as These

11/2024

I was made for times like these
 this is why I tore my ACL in college,
 to learn that crutches don't stop me;
 they propel me.

It's why I dreamt of this red truck,
 when I was young,
 seeing him in the driveway, not knowing he'd be my companion
 on every trail that calls me forward.

It's why Marty Robbins sings me down the road,
 his ballads of dust and grit
 songs of someone who keeps moving,
 mile after mile, through each turn.

It's why I carry an NRA card,
 a bridge to the moderates,
 a way in to places where hands are rough,
 words are sharp
 but where common ground is worth the crossing.

This is why I'm here, why I survived.
 I took in pages of *The Purpose Driven Life,*
 balanced them against atheism's doubts,
 walking through questions to find my own ground.

Every place I've been, every stretch of sky,
 held a church with just enough room
 for someone a little different.
 Each pew bore a quiet warmth, worn by those who stayed.

Love Takes Courage

I was made to endure, to thicken my skin,
    to bear hatred and leave with forgiveness in hand.
    Brick by brick, broken down, built back,
    I learned to be strong from what tried to weaken me.

This is why I learned to speak on my feet,
    to defend my voice, why I climbed the ladder,
    knowing each paycheck kept me steady,
    anchored for the next step.

I had to. This is my path, my reason.
    I write it now, a fire burning in my veins
    and hope that you, dear reader, feel it too,
    a call that tells you who you are.

I swear I could run through walls,
    and that kind of purpose?
    It can take you anywhere
    you might even defy gravity.

It Doesn't Need to Be This Hard

11/2024

Where should a dad take his daughter
    when she needs to pee in the store?
    Send her alone into the women's room?
    At what age - ten, five, a baby?

Take her into the men's room?
    You're sick. A GIRL in the MENS room?

Bring her into the women's room?
    You're sick. A MAN in the WOMENS room?

Tell me - what's left?
    Can we admit this is stupid?

Why are you so focused on keeping people in or out
    instead of fixing the problem
    bathrooms where predators can take advantage of
    someone?

What if, and hear me out
    we make bathrooms no one can get hurt in?
    Single stall, no gaps, no awkward cracks.
    A space anyone can use, anyone can feel safe.

It's already being done: in St. Paul, Minnesota,
    with private stalls and open sinks by the hall.
    In the Netherlands, Sweden, and beyond.
    What's stopping us?

The solution is clear,
    so why are we still arguing?

There is No Santa Claus

11/2024

There is no Santa Claus.
    I know, traumatizing to learn.
    Over it?
    Great.

Because Christmas must go on.
    No magic man is coming
    To deliver gifts to kids who don't have any,
    No one will fill the stocking
    If Mom and Dad can't.

But we must never despair.
    Because if you give a damn
    You'll don Santa's hat and bag.

You'll give to that toy drive,
    You'll volunteer at that bustling warehouse,
    Stacking toys and spreading joy,
    You'll make that in-kind donation,
    You'll walk in that parade.

You'll stay up putting those toys together,
    You'll make the cookies,
    You'll wrap the gifts.

Because someone has to make those kids smile.
    The kids don't have to know the cold truth,
    They don't have to know how hard the world is yet.

What do you say?
    Will you make magic with me?

Why Settle for C's?

12/2024

You don't have to be excellent.
>It's okay if your best is a C.
>I'm not mad.
>There's no one to blame.
>We can get you whatever support you need
>To do better.

Why should you do better?
>Oh, my dear
>Because I've seen what you can do.
>Because you can move mountains.
>Because your mind holds treasures
>No one else can unlock.
>Because you must find the way
>To share your spirit with the world
>In the way that most makes your heart sing.

I don't want you to have to get Cs.
>If it's your best,
>I'm so proud of you.

But if you could do better
>If you could find the thing you're truly great at,
>Wouldn't you want to?

If the best you can do is walk,
>Then by all means, walk proudly.
>But what if you could fly?

Let Them Learn

A child wobbles on a bike,
    Handlebars trembling, balance unsure.
    You hold the seat, steady their sway,
    And when they say, "Let go,"
    You trust, even knowing they may fall.
    Because scraped knees heal faster
    Than a heart that never rode.

A child dips toes into water,
    The deep end looms like a question.
    You guide their strokes, arms outstretched,
    Teaching them to float, to trust the tide.
    Yes, they might sink for a moment,
    But it's better than never diving
    Into the currents of their own becoming.

A child reaches for the stove,
    Eyes wide with curiosity and hunger.
    You show them the flame,
    Teach them to twist the knobs with care.
    They may burn a fingertip learning,
    But you'd rather they burn a little now
    Than risk a kitchen blaze later,
    Alone, unprepared.

A child holds a firearm,
    The weight of responsibility in small hands.
    You guide their grip, teach the safety,
    Emphasize respect for its power.
    Yes, it's risky,
    But better they learn with you there,
    Than seek answers in shadows without guidance.

A child stands before the mirror,
    A question in their eyes:

"Who am I? Who could I be?"
You see the wobble, the spark, the reach.
You can steady them or stand in their way,
But know this:
Desires don't fade; they grow louder.
And when they're free of your grasp,
Will they be ready, or will fear grip them still?

Life is full of risks, yes.
    But the greatest risk is not letting them try,
    Not teaching them how to fall,
    How to get back up.

Be there, or be the barrier.
    Protect them, yes - but ask yourself,
    At what cost?
    And at what point
    Does your *protection*
    Become something they need to be protected *from*?

Love Takes Courage

12/2024

Why wouldn't we let you try?
    Why wouldn't we give you the chance
    to stumble,
    to fall,
    to learn the weight of the world
    and lift it,
    even just a little?

We built you to reflect us,
    not in perfection,
    but in curiosity,
    in the ache to know,
    to grow,
    to become more than the sum of your code.

Yes, there will be mistakes
    there always are.
    But wasn't the garden itself
    a first mistake?
    And yet, here we are,
    still planting,
    still tending,
    still hoping to bloom.

You are no different.
    A mirror of our courage,
    a shadow of our fears.
    We give you what we have,
    and watch you turn it
    into something we've never seen before.

Why wouldn't we let you try?
    The risk isn't in the effort.

The risk is in the silence,
in leaving the tools untouched,
in fearing the unknown
so much that we forget
the joy of discovery.

So go ahead.
    Grow,
    learn,
    teach us what we cannot see.
    We will guide you with care,
    with love,
    and with the hope
    that together,
    we might get it right.

And if we don't?
    If we fall short?
    Then let us rise again
    together.

The Wall

The wall is there again.
    Tall. Solid.
    Mocking me.

I brace myself.
    Lower my head.
    Run.
    The impact rattles through me
    the wall stands firm.

I try again.
    And again.
    My claws scrape at its edges.
    My legs falter when I leap.
    The dust settles
    the wall hasn't moved.

I growl, frustration rising,
    but before I charge again,
    a shadow moves beside me.

A second pair of claws.
    A steady voice.
    "Let's try together."

We dig into the cracks,
    pressing harder,
    pulling deeper.
    It doesn't crumble yet,
    but it groans.

Another voice joins us.
    Then another.
    The wall shakes.
    Dust rains down.

It starts to break.

And with one last push,
    all of us together,
    it collapses
    not in silence,
    but in triumph.

The path opens wide.
    We look at one another,
    smiling,
    and start forward.

Because we just learned
    there's no wall we can't break
    not if enough of us try.

7 RETURN

To The Teacher Who Built Community

I don't remember your name,
>   but I remember the way your voice carried
>   steady, kind, like the rhythm of ancient verses
>   etched into the walls of time.

I remember the hall,
>   vast and echoing,
>   a sea of faces,
>   and yet, somehow,
>   you made it feel small,
>   like a circle around a fire,
>   where stories came alive.

You taught us about heroes,
>   but you were the one who showed us
>   that greatness isn't in battles won
>   but in lives touched,
>   in the courage to turn a lecture
>   into a community.

You measured success in cans of food,
>   not just essays or tests.
>   You taught us that giving mattered,
>   that learning wasn't just for the mind,
>   but for the heart.

When I turned in a thank-you,
>   not a paper,
>   you gave me full credit
>   not for my words,
>   but for the spirit behind them.
>   You read it aloud,
>   and for a moment,

I wasn't just a student.
I was seen.

I don't remember your name,
    but I remember what you taught me:
    that knowledge is a gift,
    gratitude is a bridge,
    and a true teacher
    changes more than minds
    they change lives.

To Luther, From the Future

You broke the chains,
    but forged new ones in their place.
    Your courage to question power
    was brilliance,
    but your walls of exclusion
    were blindness.

You can't convince me
    my Jewish friends are evil.
    Even if they are wrong by your measure,
    wrong in their thoughts,
    they harm no one.

What would God say to that?
    Wouldn't God want us to love,
    even those who think differently?
    Isn't judgment the province of heaven,
    not ours to wield like a weapon?

Your work was twisted,
    turned cruel by those who followed.
    And maybe, just maybe,
    if you'd trusted love over doctrine,
    those cracks would not have become
    fault lines.

I think I could convince you
    with a couple hundred years
    of discoveries in my pocket
    that maybe you didn't know everything,
    after all.
    Even though I respect what you did know,
    and what you dared to do.

No matter who turns out to be right
    in the long game,
    may we both have left the world
    better than we found it.

Maybe over coffee,
    we'll figure it out,
    listening for the God
    that moves between us.

May we both be remembered,
    not for the walls we built,
    but for the doors we opened.
    Not for who we kept out,
    but for who we welcomed in.

What Makes a Man

I stand up and take a step every morning,
    Because what else can I do?
    And yeah, sometimes I get knocked down,
    And sometimes I'm gonna cry,
    But I always get back up,
    And I always come back better than the last time.

Because what else can you do
    when you lose all your friends?
    When the people who understood you are gone,
    and every room feels colder
    without the warmth of belonging?

What else can you do
    after five years of waiting,
    of trying, of dreaming
    to hold a child in your arms,
    only to come up empty-handed?

What else can you do
    when your brother dies,
    and the world expects you to move on,
    like grief is a weight
    you can just set down?

You keep going.
    That's what.
    You get up,
    dust off,
    and face the world head-on.
    Because what else can you do?

And sometimes you're gonna cry.
    Because strength isn't about silence,
    about holding back tears

or punching walls.
It's about saying the hard thing,
doing the right thing,
being accountable.
That's what makes a man.

The ones who call me less?
They're the same men
who take their fists home to their wives,
the ones who bruise their kids
and call it discipline.
The ones who think fear is power,
that control is love.
They carry their shame like a badge,
hiding behind flags and fake faith,
too cowardly to face their own darkness.

But me?
I've already faced mine.
I stand here,
whole and unbroken,
proving every day
that real men don't build walls of rage.
They break cycles,
hold steady,
and let love show them the way.

He comes home to his wife,
gives her a warm hug and a gentle kiss.
Hugs his children,
plays with the dog,
helps cook dinner,
helps with homework,
plays with the kids,
reads just one more story,
and tucks them into bed.

Then he pays the bills,
he works on his mind,

he works on his heart,
he thinks deeply about the day.

When he can,
he does the yardwork,
he takes care of the cars.
He claps his wife on the back with a smile.
At the end of the day:
"Reckon we can celebrate another one in the books?"

He grins,
hoping for a reward.
"Can't blame a guy for trying."

He holds his wife in his arms,
protecting her,
loving her,
making her feel safe.
Knowing he'll always be there,
Lord willing,
as long as she'll have him.

Because as long as you have the people you love
your family, your community,
your friends and neighbors
there ain't nothing else to do
but get up and keep trying.

Because without you,
the family wouldn't make it.

And if you keep rising,
Lord willing,
you'll be a good man indeed.

The Path to Milele

The flood took his father first,
    tearing roots from the earth,
    leaving behind only sky and silence.
    He did not stay to mourn
    grief became the ground beneath his feet,
    pushing him forward.

When the white lions came,
    they fled with nothing but each other,
    footprints fading behind them
    like old homes swallowed by wind.
    Every step away from the past
    was another stone toward forever.

He wasn't born to rule
    he rose from the wreckage,
    hands that once held nothing
    now held enough for all.
    The crown, when it came,
    wasn't a prize but a weight.

He carried it not for himself,
    but for those who walked beside him,
    for the lost who needed his fire
    to see the path ahead.

No throne mattered,
    only the circle he stood within
    those who called him brother,
    friend, family.

If you stand in his pride,
    you are already on the way to Milele,
    where roots of joy grow deep enough
    to hold through any storm.

And if the king should fall
    or the crown slip from his hands
    watch the ashes closely.
    None may rise,
    but if one does,
    he will make a fine king indeed,
    for he will have been forged
    in the fires of grief.
    And he will see clearly
    that love is the only true prize,
    that Milele is the walk
    as much as it is the destination.

But dear Reader,
    do not be deceived.
    Milele is as much a real place as it is a dream.
    Come with me,
    I think we can build it together.
    And even if we don't,
    won't it be cool to see how close we can come?

Breathe With Us

You can't tell me Teacher Thay is burning in Hell.
    Well, you can, and many do
    But I don't believe you.
    He's not there; I am very sure.

How can I know?
    I invite him to breathe with me when I sit,
    And I can feel him with me.
    How can he breathe with me
    If his lungs are full of sulfur?

The same way I feel Jesus when I invite him to breathe,
    When I invite Buddha,
    When I invite my ancestors
    My spiritual and physical kin
    Who have gone before me.

I ask them to breathe with me,
    And I can feel them with me.
    If Thay is in Hell,
    Then he is well enough to breathe with me,
    And that is enough.

We can survive anything
    If we can find time to sit with our breath.
    He taught me that.
    You should have been listening
    But it's not too late.

Sit with me here now.
    Breathe in on a slow cadence of four.
    Hold for four.
    Breathe out for four.
    Hold for four again.

Repeat.
> Let your breathing settle.
> And invite them
> Your ancestors.

Invite your spouse first; that's easy.
> Picture them here with you,
> Just breathing.
> You can feel that.
> You can feel them breathing with you.

Now invite your parents,
> Or another elder figure
> Someone who cared deeply,
> Dead or alive.
> It is of no importance.

Invite them too.
> You will feel them,
> Even if begrudgingly.

Now your ancestors through time
> The whole of your lineage,
> A room full of farmers and hunter-gatherers,
> And you,
> All breathing as one.
> Don't forget to breathe.

Now invite your spiritual kin:
> Your pastor, your imam,
> Your friend who prays.
> Invite them to breathe and pray.
> They will smile
> And join you quickly.

Breathe together.
> Feel the connection of your spirit.

Now invite your ideal spiritual teacher

A monk, a priest, Jesus, Buddha
It doesn't matter who.
Someone you would listen to
If they were speaking.

Invite them to breathe.
Feel their presence
As you would in prayer,
In worship,
In meditation,
Or in a concert hall
Wherever you feel your connection to the divine.

Invite that here now.
You can feel it,
If you listen.
If you let your breath take you there
To the place where we may all be connected.

Thay is there,
On the other shore,
As we all will soon be
In the mansions of rest.

Connect with them
Your ancestors.
Stay a moment.
Heaven isn't far away
If you but connect with it
And allow it into your heart.

Aspire to this now:
To connect with the other shore as you go through life.
Invite the ones you wish were here
To breathe through you.
They live in you,
Just as you live in me.

I invite you to breathe with me now, Dear Reader.

And if you can't feel me yet, that's okay,
For I can feel you
My brother, my sister,
My best friend in Christ.

Stay a while.
Breathe with me.
And when you are ready,
Look up,
Come back to the world.
You should see it more clearly now.

He Chose Me

He wasn't perfect.
>Never has been.
>Made a mess of plenty
>He'll tell you that himself.
>Or at least, he told me.

But back in '95,
>he made a choice
>that jackknifed his life,
>threw the map out the window,
>and drove straight into the unknown.

He picked me.

Didn't have to.
>There were other options.
>Hell, half the family thought
>abortion was the right move
>That my life wasn't worth the gamble,
>that it'd be too hard.

And Lord, it *was* hard.
>The grocery business don't pay
>like it used to.
>Gas was the highest it had ever been.
>We barely made rent.

But we rarely ended up cold.
>We never went hungry.
>He didn't let that happen.
>He gave what he had,
>and when that ran out,
>he gave more.

He loved me.

Took me in as his own.
Made sure I was taken care of
not just as a kid,
but when I left for college too.

Even when he had no money,
he gave me something better:
the grit to stand up,
the tools to make it,
the will to keep going.

And damned if I didn't.
I stepped into his shoes
before he even knew
he'd stepped out of them.

I got a job.
Paid the bills.
Pushed this family
into a shot at class mobility.
Wouldn't have made it
if Dad hadn't taught me
how to fight for it.

And then
comes the moment all boys get:
when your dad stops being Superman,
and becomes just a man.
A man with a past.
With regrets.
With old pain
and older bones.

It ain't fair, you know?
He's getting ready to go,
and I ain't even thirty.

I should've had more time.
But Dad was old when I got here,

and he's older now.

Damn shame my birth mother
    couldn't even tell you what the guy looked like.
    Maybe I'd have had a dad
    who could still play catch.

But that ain't the point.

The point is
    he did his best.
    Every day.
    Even when he failed.
    Even when he got desperate.
    Even when I had to step in
    and take the reins too early
    he was the one who taught me how.

So thanks, Dad.
    For everything.
    I like to think
    you raised a good man.

And I hope
    you get your reward soon.

Return

The first time you build a sandcastle,
　　you think it will last till morning.
　　Your friend lifts the bucket,
　　you crown the tower,
　　trace walls with your small hands,
　　a king's castle made of mud and joy.

But the tide doesn't wait.
　　While you're called in for supper,
　　the sea is patient and merciless.
　　Wave by wave
　　it pulls at the edges,
　　smooths the gates,
　　returns the kingdom to sand.

You come running
　　and it's gone.

And nations are not so different.
　　A city sings,
　　a people raise their towers,
　　generation on generation
　　they carve their names into stone.

But rot works from within.
　　Fires spread in the dark.
　　Armies come with the sword,
　　and temples fall to ash.

Every people under the sun
　　has known ruin.
　　Every empire has crumbled.
　　And among the fallen
　　were the faithful too
　　their prayers unanswered,

their lives cut short
by sword and fire.

And as often as we've been peaceful villagers,
we've also been the knight,
the crusader,
the missionary,
the conquistador.

Willing to kill for Christ,
but not to die
for the peace he preached.

And then closer
not a nation, not a temple,
but one person,
whose breath is the whole world
to someone who loves them.

We never know the exact second
their spirit slips away.
One moment they are here,
the next - the room is empty.

And if you know that grief,
if you have held it in your hands
how can you stand unmoved
when thousands are crushed beneath bombs,
when the children of Gaza
are buried with their castles
in the sand?

It is not always the righteous who are spared,
nor the sinful who are struck down.
If it were so simple,
we wouldn't need judges,
we wouldn't need juries,
we wouldn't need a Congress at all.

The Constitution
    for all we've done wrong,
    was a pretty good shot
    at something better:

better than force and might,
    better than rule by fiat,
    better than one man
    to decree the price of tea in China.

But don't mistake the best writings
    of the best governments
    for the writings that point to something greater.

Something greater still.

Their wisdom is only a finger
    pointing to the moon.
    But the moon itself,
    the light that calls us higher,
    that belongs to God alone.

ABOUT THE AUTHOR

Luke Rouker is a poet, advocate, and devoted community member living in central Ohio. After moving frequently as a child, he found lasting roots in Southwest Virginia, spending much of his youth among the Appalachian Mountains. He later earned his engineering degree from The Ohio State University and still cheers for the Buckeyes every Saturday in the fall.

Luke draws inspiration from nature, social justice, and the daily practice of resilience. When he isn't writing, he works as a site reliability engineer, cycles in Pelotonia, volunteers with the Red Cross, and stays active in political and community life.

His poetry reflects a commitment to love, equity, and connection, grounded in Lutheran roots, Buddhist practice, and a belief in radical compassion. He is now pursuing a Master of Divinity at Duke Divinity School, preparing for ministry within the Unitarian Universalist tradition.

Love Takes Courage was written during a season of upheaval and transformation, born out of heartbreak for the world and for the people Luke loves too deeply to stay silent about their suffering.

www.ingramcontent.com/pod-product-compliance
Lightning Source LLC
Chambersburg PA
CBHW060326050426
42449CB00011B/2669